WEEKLY WR READER
EARLY LEARNING LIBRARY

Where People Work

What Happens at a

Firehouse?

by Kathleen Pohl

Reading consultant: Susan Nations, M.Ed., author/literacy coach/consultant in literacy development

Please visit our web site at: www.garethstevens.com
For a free color catalog describing Weekly Reader® Early Learning Library's list
of high-quality books, call 1-877-445-5824 (USA) or 1-800-387-3178 (Canada).
Weekly Reader® Early Learning Library's fax: (414) 336-0164.

Library of Congress Cataloging-in-Publication Data

Pohl, Kathleen.
    What happens at a firehouse? / by Kathleen Pohl.
      p. cm. — (Where people work)
    Includes bibliographical references and index.
    ISBN-10: 0-8368-6887-0 — ISBN-13: 978-0-8368-6887-6 (lib. bdg.)
    ISBN-10: 0-8368-6894-3 — ISBN-13: 978-0-8368-6894-4 (softcover)
    1. Fire stations—Juvenile literature. 2. Fire prevention—Vocational guidance—
Juvenile literature. I. Title. II. Series: Pohl, Kathleen. Where people work.
TH9148.P585   2006
628.9'25—dc22   2006008666

This edition first published in 2007 by
Weekly Reader® Early Learning Library
A Member of the WRC Media Family of Companies
330 West Olive Street, Suite 100
Milwaukee, Wisconsin 53212 USA

Buddy® is a registered trademark of Weekly Reader Corporation. Used under license.

Managing editor: Dorothy L. Gibbs
Art direction: Tammy West
Cover design and page layout: Scott M. Krall
Picture research: Diane Laska-Swanke and Kathleen Pohl
Photographer: Jack Long

Acknowledgments: The publisher thanks the Milwaukee Fire Department for its kind cooperation
and assistance in publishing this book. Special thanks to Lt. Brian O'Connor and the firefighters of
Engine 18 (David Ciszewski, Richard Conard, Jermaine Ebo, James Elz, Kurt LeRoy, Anthony Lewis,
Robert Lewis, Thomas Locke, Thomas McMenamin, and Scott Terris) for their expert consulting and
for appearing in the photographs.

Printed in the United States of America

1 2 3 4 5 6 7 8 9 10 09 08 07 06

Hi, Kids!

I'm Buddy, your Weekly Reader® pal. Have you ever visited a firehouse? I'm here to show and tell what happens at a firehouse. So, come on. Turn the page and read along!

A firehouse is like a family's house! **Firefighters** live here so they will be ready to fight fires. They stay one or two days at a time.

One firefighter cooks the meals. Everyone eats at a long table — like a big family!

One firefighter cooks the meals. Everyone eats at a long table — like a big family!

The firefighters sleep in one big room. It has many beds. Sometimes, they take naps here, too.

The firehouse has a big garage with big fire trucks inside. The trucks are always clean and shiny.

The firefighters wash
the trucks after every fire.
They even wash the **hoses**.

hose

They clean their **helmets**. They clean and check their **masks**. The masks help them breathe when they are fighting fires.

mask

helmet

Firefighters wear special clothes and boots to fight fires. They put their clothes by the fire trucks to be ready.

The **fire alarm** goes off. It is very loud! The firefighters quickly check a computer and a map. They need to find out where the fire is.

Now they have to move fast! They pull on their special clothes. They jump into their boots. They hop on the trucks. Get out of the way, everybody!

 # Glossary

fire alarm — a loud sound that lets firefighters know there is a fire somewhere

firefighters — men and women who are trained to fight fires

helmets — hard hats people wear to keep their heads safe

hoses — big, long tubes that water flows through so it can be sprayed on fires

masks — coverings for the face that give the people wearing them air to breathe

🐻 For More Information

Books

Firefighter. People in My Community (series). Jacqueline
   Laks Gorman (Gareth Stevens)

A Visit to a Fire Station. B. A. Hoena (Pebble Plus)

What's Inside a Firehouse? What's Inside? (series).
   Sharon Gordon (Benchmark Books)

Web Site

Kid's Firehouse
   www.diamondstarfire.org/3.html
   Become a junior fire marshall and learn how to keep
   your home safe from fires.

Publisher's note to educators and parents: Our editors have
carefully reviewed this Web site to ensure that it is suitable for children.
Many Web sites change frequently, however, and we cannot guarantee
that a site's future contents will continue to meet our high standards of
quality and educational value. Be advised that children should be closely
supervised whenever they access the Internet.

 # Index

About the Author

Kathleen Pohl has written and edited many children's books. Among them are animal tales, rhyming books, retold classics, and the forty-book series *Nature Close-Ups*. She also served for many years as top editor of *Taste of Home* and *Country Woman* magazines. She and her husband, Bruce, live among beautiful Wisconsin woods and share their home with six goats, a llama, and all kinds of wonderful woodland creatures.